What's Inside
Submarines

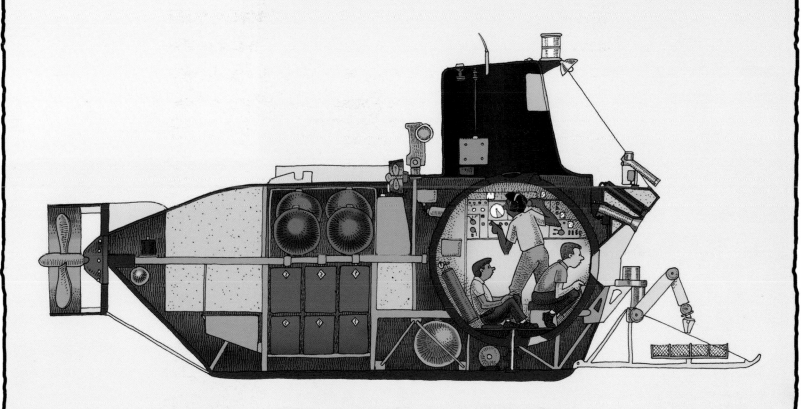

W

FRANKLIN WATTS
LONDON•SYDNEY

Franklin Watts
First published in Great Britain in 2016 by The Watts Publishing Group

Copyright © 2015 David West Children's Books

All rights reserved.

Designed and illustrated by David West

Dewey number 623.8'257-dc23
HB ISBN 978 1 4451 4622 5

Printed in Malaysia

Franklin Watts
An imprint of
Hachette Children's Group
Part of The Watts Publishing Group
Carmelite House
50 Victoria Embankment
London EC4Y 0DZ

An Hachette UK Company
www.hachette.co.uk

www.franklinwatts.co.uk

WHAT'S INSIDE SUBMARINES
was produced for Franklin Watts by
David West 🯅🯆 Children's Books, 6 Princeton Court, 55 Felsham Road, London SW15 1AZ

Contents

The First Submarines

The first successful submarine was built in 1620. It was powered by oars and had tubes attached to floats to supply air. The first military submarines were built in the 1700s. The American "Turtle", built in 1776, was designed by David Bushnell. It used a hand-operated propeller to move. It attempted to blow up a British warship but failed to attach its **mine**.

Bushnell's Turtle looked like a barrel. It was operated by one man. A detachable explosive mine was attached to a large screw. This was screwed into the enemy ship's hull and released along with the mine.

Bushnell's Turtle

Breathing tube
This lets air in when it is above the water level.

Detachable mine
The explosive charge can be released once it is attached to the hull of a ship.

Rudder
This is used to steer the Turtle.

Pump
Water can be pumped in or out of the ballast tank.

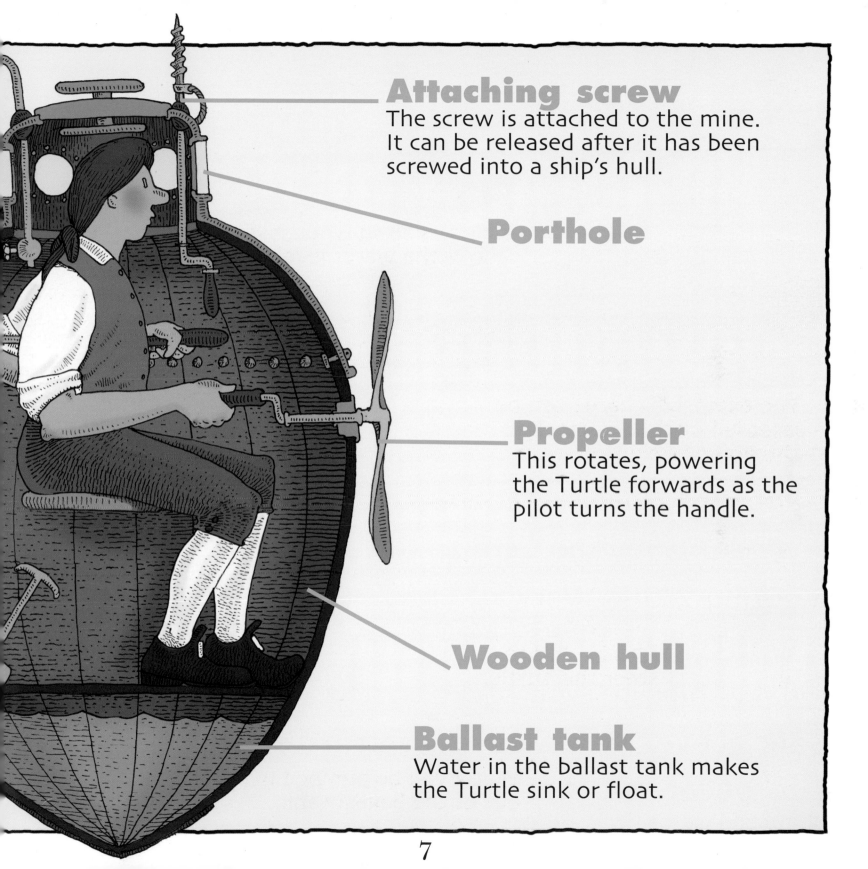

Attaching screw
The screw is attached to the mine. It can be released after it has been screwed into a ship's hull.

Porthole

Propeller
This rotates, powering the Turtle forwards as the pilot turns the handle.

Wooden hull

Ballast tank
Water in the ballast tank makes the Turtle sink or float.

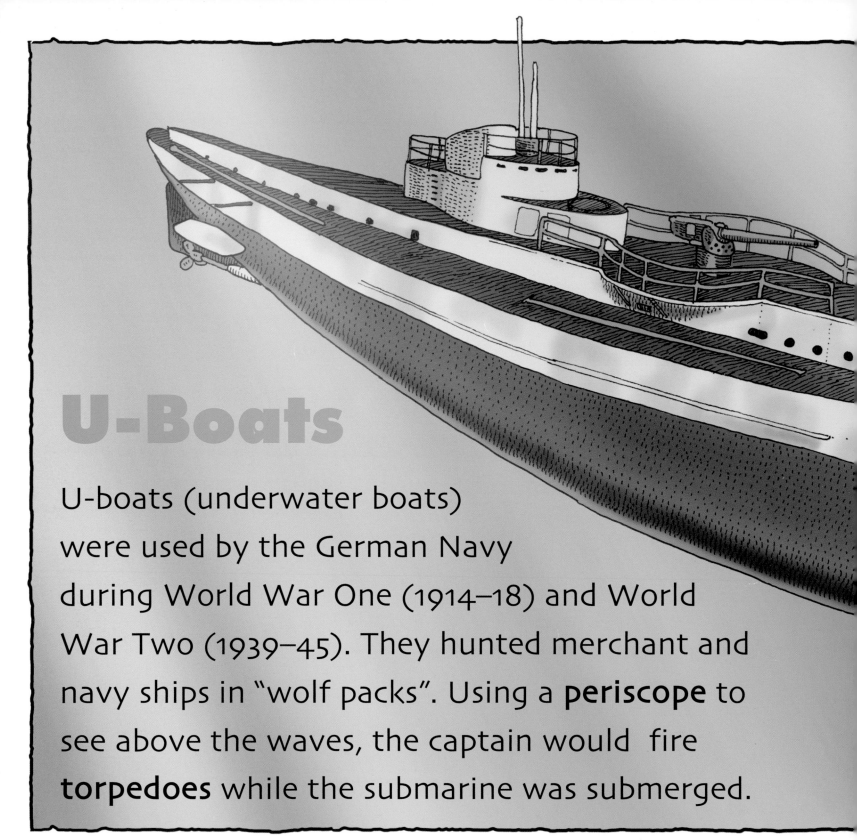

U-Boats

U-boats (underwater boats) were used by the German Navy during World War One (1914–18) and World War Two (1939–45). They hunted merchant and navy ships in "wolf packs". Using a **periscope** to see above the waves, the captain would fire **torpedoes** while the submarine was submerged.

Submarines like this World War One U-boat could only dive to around 90 metres. Later World War Two U-boats could dive to more than 300 metres.

U-Boat U 81

Inner hull
The inner hull withstands the pressure of the water when the U-boat dives.

Bunks

Rear torpedo room

Oxygen tanks

Control room
The U-boat is steered and commanded from here.

Propeller

Rudder

Fuel tank

Electric motor
When it is underwater, the U-boat uses the electric motors.

Diesel engine
A diesel engine powers the U-boat when it is surfaced.

Periscopes

Conning tower

This houses the periscopes. It is also where the captain and officers stand when the boat is surfaced.

Outer hull

This contains ballast tanks to allow the U-boat to surface and dive. Water is forced out by air from oxygen tanks to make the U-boat rise.

Oxygen tanks

Gun

The gun is used for firing at enemy ships when the U-boat is surfaced.

Hatch

Bunks

Fresh water tank

Forward torpedo room

Torpedoes are loaded into tubes and fired towards enemy ships.

Galley

This is where the crew eat.

Batteries

Batteries supply electricity for the electric motors and the U-boat's electronics.

Midget Submarines

Most midget submarines were used during World War Two to attack battleships in harbours. They were operated by crews of two to four men. They usually worked with **motherships**, which towed them a distance before letting them loose on their target.

This British X-class submarine had a diver as part of the crew. If there were anti-submarine nets, the diver could get out and cut a hole in them. Large mines on each side, with time fuses, were dropped under enemy ships.

X-Class Submarine

Electric motor
The electric motor is used when the submarine is underwater.

Rudder and hydroplane control

Hatch

Rudder

Hydroplane

Oxygen cylinders

Propeller

Diesel engine
This engine is used when the submarine is surfaced.

Gyro compass
This shows which way the submarine is pointing.

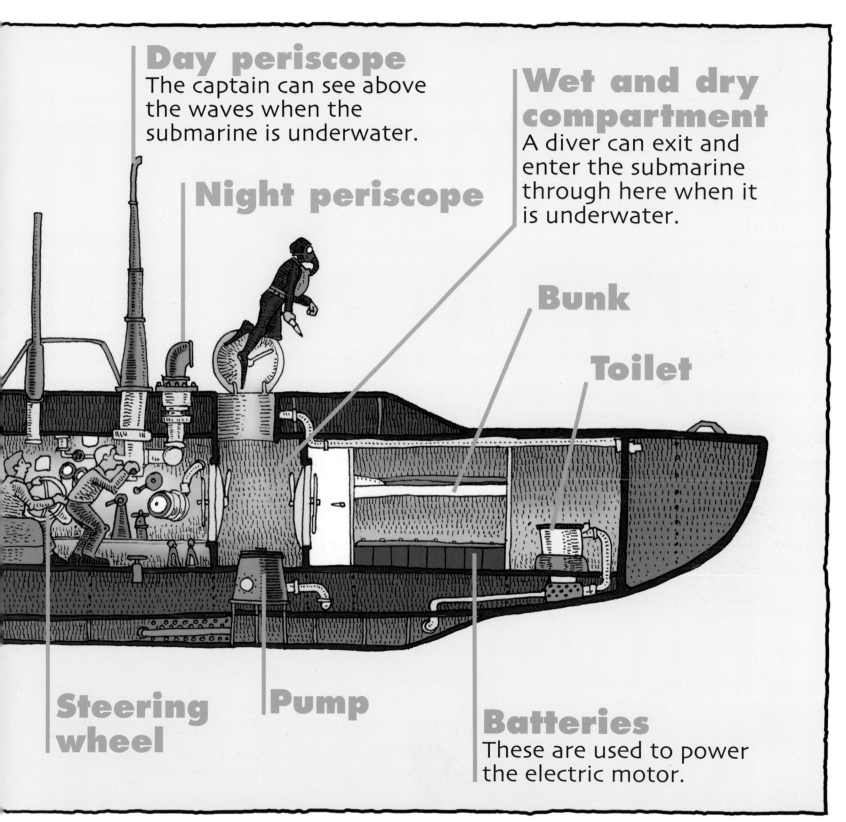

Day periscope
The captain can see above the waves when the submarine is underwater.

Night periscope

Wet and dry compartment
A diver can exit and enter the submarine through here when it is underwater.

Bunk

Toilet

Steering wheel

Pump

Batteries
These are used to power the electric motor.

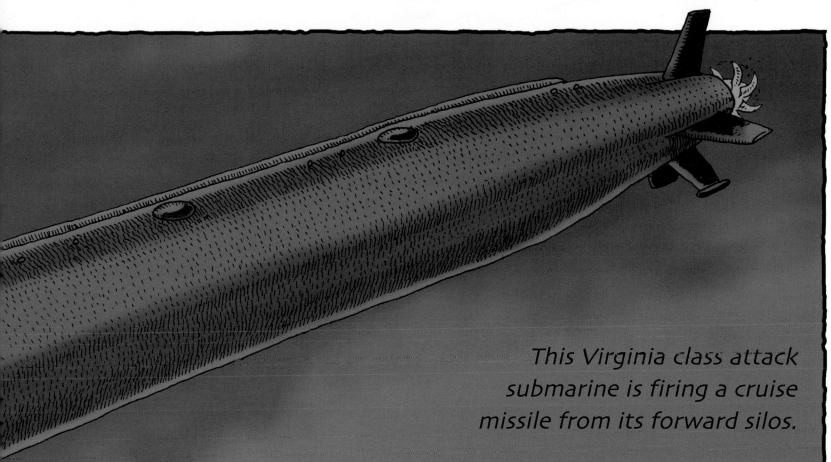

This Virginia class attack submarine is firing a cruise missile from its forward silos.

Modern Submarines

Modern submarines are usually powered by a **nuclear reactor**. This means they can stay under the water for months at a time. They can fire missiles as well as torpedoes and use clever electronics and **sonar** to detect enemy vessels.

Nuclear Submarine

Propeller

Nuclear reactor
The submarine is powered by a nuclear reactor that produces steam to power the turbines.

Generators
These provide electricity for the submarine and the electric motor.

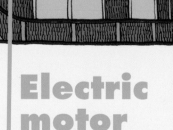

Electric motor

Turbines
Steam from the nuclear reactor turns turbines, which power generators.

Steering fins

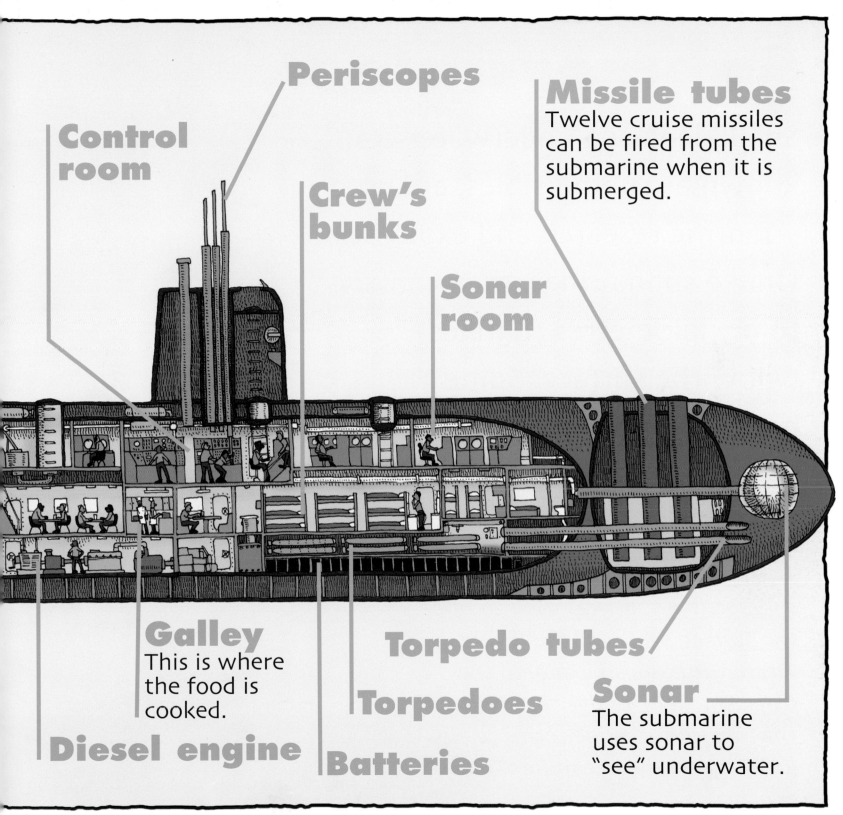

Control room

Periscopes

Crew's bunks

Sonar room

Missile tubes
Twelve cruise missiles can be fired from the submarine when it is submerged.

Galley
This is where the food is cooked.

Diesel engine

Torpedo tubes

Torpedoes

Batteries

Sonar
The submarine uses sonar to "see" underwater.

Submersibles

Small deep-sea underwater craft, known as submersibles, are used for scientific research and exploration. Unlike submarines, they can dive to 9.7 kilometres (6 miles) below the surface. Some have remote-controlled arms to collect samples.

The DSV Alvin is a well-known submersible that was used to find the sunken wreck of the RMS Titanic. It has also explored the black smokers, underwater vents that support strange forms of life deep on the ocean floor.

DSV Alvin

Propeller and electric motor
This is the main power for the submersible.

Buoyancy material

Pressurised air spheres
These spheres provide air for the ballast tanks.

Batteries
Batteries supply power to the motors and electronics.

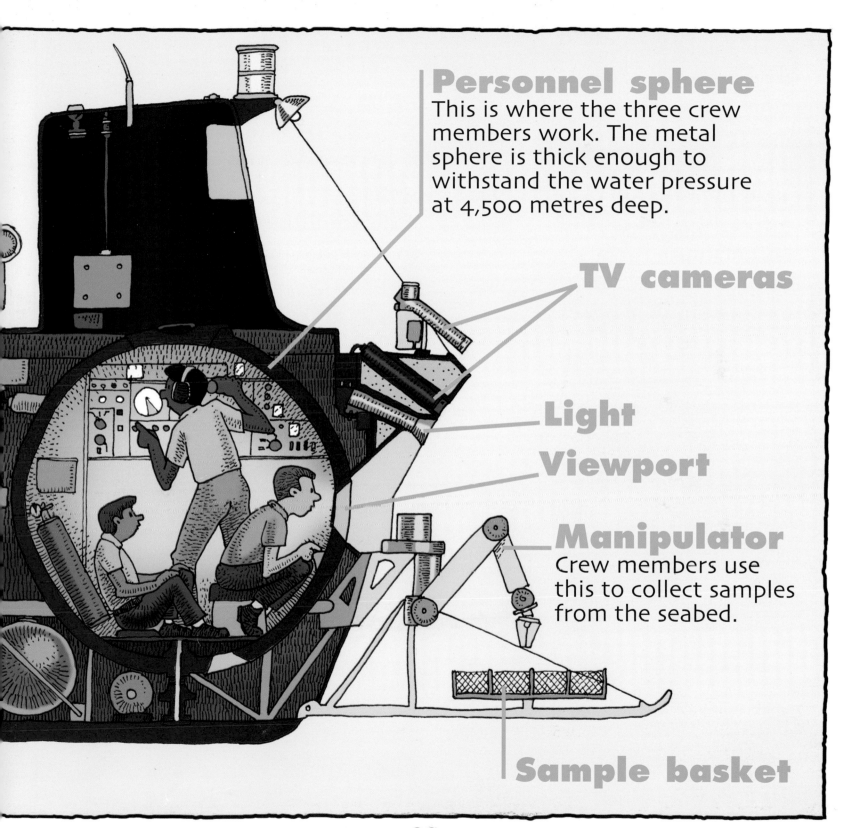

Personnel sphere
This is where the three crew members work. The metal sphere is thick enough to withstand the water pressure at 4,500 metres deep.

TV cameras

Light

Viewport

Manipulator
Crew members use this to collect samples from the seabed.

Sample basket

Glossary

mine

An explosive device used mainly at sea, which explodes after a given time period or on contact with a ship.

mothership

A ship or submarine that tows another smaller vessel.

nuclear reactor

A device that uses controlled atomic power to create heat to make steam.

periscope

A device that uses mirrors to see over the top of things.

sonar

A device that uses sound echoes to navigate underwater.

torpedo

A self-propelled underwater weapon with an explosive warhead.

Index